Returning Home: Journeys to Israel

Elisa Silverman

Voices from Israel

Mitchell Lane
PUBLISHERS
P.O. Box 196
Hockessin, Delaware 19707

Set 1
Benjamin Netanyahu

The Experience of Israel: Sights and Cities

I Am Israeli: The Children of Israel

Returning Home: Journeys to Israel

Working Together: Economy, Technology, and Careers in Israel

Set 2
Americans in the Holy Land

Culture, Customs, and Celebrations in Israel

Israel and the Arab World

Israel: Holy Land to Many

Israel: Stories of Conflict and Resolution, Love and Death

Mitchell Lane
PUBLISHERS

Copyright © 2016 by Mitchell Lane Publishers, Inc. All rights reserved. No part of this book may be reproduced without written permission from the publisher. Printed and bound in the United States of America.

Printing 1 2 3 4 5 6 7 8 9

Library of Congress Cataloging-in-Publication Data
Silverman, Elisa, author.
 Returning home : journeys to Israel / by Elisa Silverman.
    pages cm. — (Voices from Israel)
Includes bibliographical references and index.
ISBN 978-1-61228-686-0 (library bound)
1. Israel—Emigration and immigration—Juvenile literature. I. Title.
JV8749.S54 2014
 305.9'0691209225694—dc23
                                                                                           2015017401
eBook ISBN: 978-1-61228-695-2

ABOUT THE COVER: The Israeli flag, with its blue stripes, is modeled after a traditional Jewish prayer shawl. A Shield of David (or Star of David), which has no specific religious meaning, was added as the symbol of the Jewish people. The flag was created to represent the Zionist movement in 1897. The state of Israel adopted it as its own flag in 1948.

PUBLISHER'S NOTE: This story is based on the author's extensive research and knowledge of Israel, which she believes to be accurate. Documentation of such research is contained on pp. 56–60.

 The Internet sites referenced herein were active as of the publication date. Due to the fleeting nature of some web sites, we cannot guarantee they will all be active when you are reading this book.

 To reflect current usage, we have chosen to use the secular era designations BCE ("before the common era") and CE ("of the common era") instead of the traditional designations BC ("before Christ") and AD (*anno Domini,* "in the year of the Lord").

PRONUNCIATION NOTE: The author has included pronunciations for many of the Hebrew words in this book. In these pronunciations, the letters "ch" are not pronounced like the "ch" in "children." Instead, the letters "ch" represent the Hebrew letter chet, which sounds like a "kh" or hard "h" sound, similar to the "ch" in "Loch Ness Monster."

PBP

CONTENTS

Introduction 6
CHAPTER 1: Two Sisters; Two Countries 13
   Lone Soldiers in the Israeli Army 19
CHAPTER 2: A Dangerous Journey 21
   The Ancient Roots of Ethiopian Jews 27
CHAPTER 3: The Accidental Israeli 29
   The Life Adventures of a Russian Activist 35
CHAPTER 4: "Sunday People" 37
   Israel's Christian Visitors 41
CHAPTER 5: The Beauty of a Challenging Life 43
   A Chapter in French History—The Dreyfus Affair 47
CHAPTER 6: From Tehran to Tel Aviv 49
   Hidden Jews 53

Chapter Notes 54
Works Consulted 56
Further Reading 60
On the Internet 60
Glossary 61
Index 63

BOLD words in the text can be found in the glossary.

Introduction

"Next year in Jerusalem!" Every Passover *seder* (seh-dehr), a special meal central to Jewish identity, ends with these words. Each spring, Jews retell the story of the Israelites escaping slavery in Egypt, crossing the desert and building their own nation. The **exclamation** "Next Year in Jerusalem" symbolizes the yearning of the Jews to return to their ancient homeland, lost to them nearly two thousand years ago.

In the Beginning

The earliest Jewish nation in Israel was established around 1020 BCE. After 400 years of Jewish kingdoms in the Land of Israel, the Jews were conquered and suffered their first expulsion from their land. Since this first **ouster**, the Jewish people dreamt of returning to their land. Fortunately, new rulers, the Persians, let them return. Thus the Jews were able to rebuild the **Holy Temple** in Jerusalem that the Babylonians had destroyed. However, not all the Jews who had been forced to leave returned to Israel.

Israel Museum's scale model of Jerusalem, circa 66 CE. The large four-walled complex at the center is the Second Temple, which was destroyed by the Romans in 70 CE. Today only a portion of the Temple's Western Wall remains standing.

One of Judaism's central prayers, the *Shmoneh Esrei* (shmoh-NEH ess-RAY), was written in the fifth century BCE by the Knesset haGadola (keh-neh-set ha-gah-dowl-ah) ("the Great Assembly"), the name given to the leaders of the Jewish community in ancient Israel. Within the Shmoneh Esrei are specific prayers for gathering the exiled Jews back to Israel and for the restoration of Jerusalem as the capital of the Jewish people. From that time until today, religious Jews have been reciting the Shmoneh Esrei prayer three times a day while facing Jerusalem.

Unfortunately, the rebuilding of Jewish life in Israel didn't last. The Romans conquered the region in 63 BCE. Jews revolted under Roman rule and in 135 CE, the Romans killed, enslaved, or expelled all the Jews living there. For the next 1,800 years or so, only a small Jewish community remained in their homeland, while the rest of the Jews were scattered throughout the world.

The Arch of Titus was built in 82 CE to celebrate Roman victories. The portion shown depicts the Roman sacking of the Second Temple and carrying off pieces of it, most notably a seven-armed candelabra. Called a menorah (meh-nawr-uh), it is a symbol of the Jewish nation and was used in the Temple. Today the menorah remains Israel's national emblem.

INTRODUCTION

Like the ancient Israelites before them, a family of Egyptian Jews arrive to Israel—this time in the twentieth century (1950).

The Ingathering of Exiles

As the land of Israel was passed from conqueror to conqueror, Jewish life continued there. Jews returned to Israel because they were drawn there by religious feeling. The eleventh century philosopher and poet **Rabbi** Yehuda Halevi wrote about the desire to return to Israel: "My heart is in the East and I am at the edge of West." The Rabbi, who was born in Spain, and his poetic words offer only one of many prayers and literary expressions of the Jewish longing for their homeland through the centuries.

In 1211, one of the earliest organized group immigrations to Israel was led by rabbis from England and France. Religiously inspired immigration to Israel continued in a small stream through the eighteenth century from Europe, North Africa, and the Middle East.

A broader movement to return to the ancient homeland of the Jewish people has its roots in more recent centuries. The French Revolution of 1789 had great impact on the Jews of Europe. European governments started lifting their oppressive laws against Jews. They opened their **ghettos** and gave their Jewish citizens full civil rights. The Jews believed they would at last be accepted as equals.

INTRODUCTION

They soon learned that this was not the case. It wasn't long before some of the old legal restrictions were renewed, separating and repressing Jews once again. As many Jews began to **assimilate** into the societies in which they lived, the nature of **anti-Semitism** began to change. In the Middle Ages, anti-Semitism was religious **persecution** for the most part. But in the nineteenth century, anti-Semitism took on a racist tone. The fact that Jews lived and worked among their fellow citizens was no barrier against hatred. For a new generation of anti-Semites, the Jews were an inferior race who could never be accepted.

Confronted with this discrimination, Jews in Europe began writing about more than religious longing. They began to write about the revival of a Jewish national life in Israel. This movement became known as **Zionism**, and its followers were known as Zionists. This movement gained strength not only in Europe, but in Russia. Zionist Russian Jews began an organized movement to return to the Land of Israel, where they would be free from the Russian armies that constantly attacked Jewish villages. In 1882, the first group of Zionist Russian Jews came to settle in Israel.

As Jewish writers and leaders became more organized, the waves of *aliyah* (ahh-lee-AH) got larger and more successful. Aliyah means "to ascend" in Hebrew, and it is the term used to describe the act of returning to the Land of Israel. The first waves of Zionist Jews who moved to Israel were mostly from Russia and Eastern Europe. Central and Western European Jews started to move to Israel in greater numbers during the period between the two World Wars.

Jews who had lived in the Middle East, Asia, and North Africa for many centuries began to return to Israel in the 1930s. By the 1970s, the Jewish communities in these countries were almost entirely gone. There have been other major waves of aliyah in more recent years. Russian Jews came to Israel in great waves after the breakup of the Soviet Union in 1991. In the 1980s, Ethiopian Jews, who had longed to return to Israel for centuries, were brought home in dramatic airlifts by the Israeli government.

The ship "The Jewish State" carried European Jewish refugees from Bulgaria to Israel in 1947. The voyage was part of Aliyah Bet, a program of illegal immigration from 1934–1948. During these years, the land of Israel was under British control. The British severely restricted the number of Jewish immigrants allowed to enter just when Jews needed most to escape Europe in the years before and during World War II. After suffering British water hoses and tear gas, "The Jewish State" and its passengers were turned away from the Haifa port and sent to an intern camp on the Mediterranean island of Cyprus.

From the earliest days of aliyah through today, Jews have decided to return to Israel for many different reasons. The nineteenth century Zionist pioneers were motivated to build a modern Jewish state on their historic land. In many cases, they fled anti-Semitism or were expelled from the countries where they lived. Other Jews decided to return to Israel because major changes in the countries where they lived created chaos, and they wanted to leave. There were also Zionists who were not in danger, but left countries where they had lived for many generations because they dreamed of living a Jewish life in the Jewish homeland.

INTRODUCTION

Some Jews who left countries in distress chose to live in other parts of the world. Many of the Jews who fled Russia in the late nineteenth century decided to move to North America, and not Israel. Nearly one million Jews fled their homes in Arab and North African countries, two-thirds of whom chose to come to Israel. Others moved to France, Canada or the United States.[1]

Over the centuries, every Jew making aliyah has chosen to live in Israel, the historic Jewish homeland. Individuals and families from across the world have their own personal stories to explain the journey that brought them to the tiny land of Israel. In this book, you'll read about two young sisters from the United States who came to Israel when their parents decided to "make aliyah." You will also learn about a French businesswoman who decided to move to Israel even though her career in France was going well. You'll also discover the story of a man who was born in Russia and came to Israel with his parents when he was a child. Each of these stories reflects a different personal experience of the return home of Israel's **olim**.

New immigrants arriving in Israel in 2007 on a flight chartered by Nefesh b'Nefesh, an organization with the mission to bring North American and British Jews to Israel.

Big sister Michal and younger sister Shira at a playground in Israel with their youngest brother, little Yehuda.

CHAPTER 1
Two Sisters; Two Countries

Shira and Michal are sisters, but they were born in different countries.[1] Older sister Michal, who is about to start high school, was born in Israel. Eight-year-old Shira was born in the United States. The family lives in Israel now, so this may all seem confusing. Except this family had lived in Israel once before. The parents, both American Jews, had made aliyah separately when they were young adults. They lived in Israel for a number of years before they met. They married and began their family. That's when Michal was born.

Their father had been married before, and the son from his first marriage moved back to the United States shortly after Michal was born. The parents decided that keeping the family together was most important, so they followed Michal's stepbrother, Raanan, back to New Jersey. However, they are a religious family and always planned to return to Israel. The parents wanted Michal, and six other children born in the United States, to live a Jewish life in the Jewish nation. Once Raanan graduated from high school, the girls' parents knew it was time to return to Israel. Their mother says, "We miss Raanan, but he's a young man now. And he comes to visit often."

Michal, Shira, and their siblings were raised with the knowledge that they would one day move to Israel. Their parents tried to prepare their children as best they could. They watched Disney films **dubbed** in Hebrew. Their father spoke to them only in Hebrew, even though he didn't speak it very well.

CHAPTER 1

A portrait of the whole family. Shira is standing against the tree, and Michal is sitting with Yehuda in her lap. They're surrounded by their parents, Barak and Rachel, and their other siblings: Yechiel, Noam, Raanan, Eitan and Zev.

Whenever the girls asked their parents to buy something big, they'd always reply, "After we get to Israel." Picking up and moving a family of seven children is no small task. Their parents wanted to travel as lightly as possible.

They also prepared the girls to understand that there are people in the world who don't like Israel or Jews, and who act violently against it. Some of these groups fire rockets into Israel, and Shira worries about this sometimes. But mostly she focuses on how much she loves Israel and being connected to her Judaism and **Hashem** (hah-SHEHM) by living there.

Leaving Home and Coming Home

In July 2013, the family returned to Israel. They now live in a small religious community outside Jerusalem. Although she heard her parents talk about the move for many years, Michal didn't really think it would happen. She says it wasn't until a month before they left that it really hit her. Shira was excited to finally move to Israel. They both remember their first night in Israel. They ate dinner in an empty house, with no furniture except a 12-year old picnic table and a few mattresses on the floor. Shira wished they had brought her bunk bed.

The girls started their new schools, which they both described as very different from their American school. First, their classes were much larger. There are about 30 children in a class, and it's very noisy. In the early days, when Shira still had trouble understanding Hebrew, she would sometimes walk out of her class and stand in the hallway. The chaos of her classroom was just too much for her.

Shira likes to study math and also enjoys learning about ancient prophets in the Hebrew Bible. Michal's favorite subject is history. Both girls also have weekly lessons with their rabbi. Michal explains that the rabbi usually has a prepared lesson, but he lets the older girls raise whatever topics they want. One week, a girl asked about dinosaurs, and they discussed how science and **Torah** may be understood in light of one another.

A classroom in the southern city of Be'er Sheva after it was hit by rockets fired out of Gaza by Hamas during Israel's 2008–2009 conflict with the terror organization.

Two Sisters; Two Countries

Field trips in Israel also proved very different from America. Michal explains that in her American school, field trips were usually to museums. In Israel, most field trips are *tiyulim* (tee-yoo-LEEM), Hebrew for hikes. Israelis love to hike and be close to the land. Shira and Michal also enjoy many activities after school. Shira especially loves animals, including snakes and lizards. Michal prefers choir and drama camp.

The Differences between Life in America and Israel

The girls worked hard to make new friends. Families don't move around that much in Israel. As a result, most of their classmates have known each other since kindergarten, and were already paired up with best friends when the girls arrived. But make friends they did, with kids from all over the world as well as those born in Israel. They generally speak Hebrew with their friends.

Kids on a school field trip, taking a hike outside Hadera, a city in northern Israel.

CHAPTER 1

For both girls, one of the biggest differences between life in Israel and the United States is that they have a lot more freedom in Israel. Michal explains that in America, if they wanted to play with friends, the parents would have to arrange it. In Israel when kids want to get together with friends, they just do it. Even Shira, who is younger, has more freedom. Both girls walk a lot more in Israel, and they can go as far away from home as they can walk.

Both girls also like the responsibility that comes with their greater freedom. Eight-year-old Shira walks on her own to their local convenience store, *makolet* (mah-KOH-let) in Hebrew. She picks up groceries on her own for the family. Michal and her friends recently had a bonfire. Although there were a few adults to keep a watchful eye, mostly the eighth graders handled it on their own.

"People here know that kids can deal with things. It feels good to be independent and without adults hovering over you all the time," Michal says.

Now that they have lived in Israel for a little more than a year, Shira and Michal notice that they are both Israeli and American. Shira likes *chummus* (khuh-moos), a spread made of chick peas, but she still really loves her ketchup. Michal says her friends don't see her as entirely American, but the sisters still feel a bit American. Israeli or American, both girls are happy to be living in *Eretz Hakodesh* (eh-REHTZ ha-koh-DESH), the Holy Land.

chummus

LONE SOLDIERS IN THE ISRAELI ARMY

A Hebrew saying heard often in Israel is *kulanu mishpacha* (koo-LAH-noo meesh-PUH-khah), "We're all family." Living that motto, Shira and Michal's family, like many others, have "adopted" one of Israel's lone soldiers.

A lone soldier is anyone serving in the Israeli army (known as the Israel Defense Forces, or IDF) who doesn't have a local family to provide support. Most lone soldiers are olim who came to Israel with the intention of serving in the military. Other lone soldiers are foreign volunteers or native-born Israelis who are orphans, or soldiers from troubled families that aren't able to give them the support they need.

The country and the military provide a range of special services to support lone soldiers. Some of the help is practical, such as providing financial assistance and an apartment where they can live when they are not on their base. They also get help with military paperwork. Of course, emotional and social support are also very important. That is why there are people who help arrange to pair them with Israeli families like Michal and Shira's, who invite them for **Shabbat** and holidays and send them care packages.

There are nearly 6,000 lone soldiers currently serving in the IDF. It is estimated that a third are American.[2] They come from all over world, and these young men and women are among Israel's most motivated soldiers. They often serve in combat and other dangerous units. Israelis want to make sure that these soldiers never feel alone. When two American lone soldiers were killed during a war between Israel and **Hamas** in 2014, their funerals were attended by between thirty and fifty thousand people.[3]

American lone soldiers enjoy Thanksgiving in 2010. Every year, the Center for American Jewry in Jerusalem invites lone soldiers for a Thanksgiving meal.

Shimon Solomon served in the Knesset from February 2013 through March 2015. During his time in parliament, he was a member of the Finance Committee, as well as the Labor, Welfare, and Health Committee. He also chaired parliamentary organizations on Ethiopian Soldiers and Strengthening the Relations Between Israel and African Countries.

CHAPTER 2
A Dangerous Journey

Ten-year-old Teshome and his family walked for weeks, on a journey of nearly 450 miles across a fearsome desert. There were thousands of other Ethiopian Jews who made a similar trek from Ethiopia to Sudan. Teshome nearly died for lack of water. Yet, Teshome, his parents, his five brothers and sisters, and the others who were with them did not give up on their difficult journey. Why? As Teshome recalls, "We always knew we were Jewish and that we would want to leave [Ethiopia]. . . . At the first opportunity to go to Israel, we will have to leave without looking back."[1]

Teshome, now an adult, is now called by a Hebrew name, Shimon (shee-mown). He grew up in Israel, where he and his family have lived since 1980. Shimon was elected a member of the *Knesset* (ki-NEH-set), Israel's parliament. He still remembers his family's dangerous, **stealthy** journey to Israel very well.

Shimon was born in the Ethiopian village of Bet Marya. In his Jewish community, the religious leaders, called *Kessim* (KESS-eem) taught them nothing was more important than returning to their ancient homeland—Israel. Unfortunately, no one was allowed to leave Ethiopia at the time. Leaving was dangerous.

A dream of many centuries was fulfilled when the State of Israel brought the Ethiopian Jewish community home. The politics in the region caused many complications, but over the

CHAPTER 2

course of a decade, most of Ethiopia's Jews were brought to Israel on **airlifts** planned by the Israeli government. Shimon's family and thousands of Ethiopian Jews spent difficult weeks in the Sudan. They had to hide their Jewish identity to try to escape **vicious** anti-Semitism. Many suffered violence, kidnapping, arrest, and **torture**. Shimon's father tried to make contact with **Mossad** to help them reach Israel. After four months of effort, the family was finally able to board a flight to Israel.

His family's first home in Israel was at an **absorption center** in the southern city of *Be'er Sheva* (beh-ear SHEH-vah). His religious family was shocked to discover that not all Israelis were religious, and many did not even observe the Sabbath. At first, it was difficult for Shimon to learn Hebrew, and he struggled in school. Later he went to school at Yemin Orde (Yeh-MEEN Ord) Youth Village. This unique school was opened in 1953 to help **Holocaust** orphans and other immigrant children adapt to life in Israel. Today it continues to assist first-generation immigrants to Israel who've experienced trauma early in life.

Like the vast majority of Israelis, Shimon served in the IDF. He became an officer in the **paratroopers** and holds the rank of major in the reserves. During his early days in the IDF, he recalls an officer who made racist comments about Ethiopians. Shimon explains how he reacted. "Had I taken the path of emotion, all I would have done is fight and get angry," he said. "Sometimes you have to suffer, and sacrifice, to get to a higher place."[2]

After he completed his military service, his focus has been supporting the Ethiopian community in Israel, as well as non-Jewish African refugees in the country. Through his work, he's retraced some of the steps he had taken during his early life.

Ethiopian immigrants arrive in Israel as part of Operation Solomon (1991), walking off of one of the 30 planes used in the operation. They were among 15,000 Ethiopians brought to Israel in a 26-hour period.

Then Prime Minister Yitzhak Shamir greets Ethiopian immigrants to Israel in 1991. The immigrants' first stop in Israel was the Hadera Absorption Center in the north.

CHAPTER 2

He returned to Ethiopia for a couple of years to represent Israel's government there. He also returned to his absorption center in Be'er Sheva as its director.

Shimon contributed to bringing the success of the Yemin Orde method to the African country of Rwanda. In 2008, he was the Director of Education at the Agahozo-Shalom Youth Village, which applied the same Yemin Orde values of education, leadership, and cultural identity he'd learned in Israel, to children who'd survived Rwanda's **genocide**.

Shimon got his first taste of politics in 2001, when he worked on the staff of the Minister of Education. He returned more than a decade later, joining a new political party *Yesh Atid* (yay-sh ah-teed), which means "there is a future." A centrist party established in 2012, two of its key priorities are improving education and boosting the economy through assistance for small businesses. With the party's success in the January 2013 elections, Shimon Solomon was sworn in as a member of the Knesset on February 5, 2013.

The Knesset building in Jerusalem where Israel's parliament meets.

THE ANCIENT ROOTS OF ETHIOPIAN JEWS

It is often difficult to know the exact origins of ancient communities. Some believe the Ethiopians are one of ancient Israel's lost tribes. Others say they are the descendants of King Solomon and the Queen of Sheba. *Beta Israel* (bay-tah yiss-RAH-el), which means "House of Israel," is the name Ethiopian Jews have given to their community, and it is believed that this Jewish community lived in Ethiopia for around two thousand years.

Prior to 1980, very few Ethiopian Jews immigrated to Israel. In the 1980s, the Israeli government began its formal, yet secret operations to bring the entire community to Israel. Ethiopia suffered from famine and political instability. Jews had been targets of anti-Semitism for centuries in Ethiopia, but their fate had gotten even worse. By 1991, the operations were out in the open. One of the most famous is Operation Solomon. The entire operation that brought 15,000 Jews to Israel took 36 hours. But first, the Israeli government paid Ethiopia's dictator a $35 million ransom to free them.

All told, the missions of the Israeli government brought around 90,000 Ethiopian Jews to Israel. The government stopped organizing group aliyah from Ethiopia in August 2013. Now, Ethiopian Jews must apply for Israeli citizenship individually, like other Jews. This policy change has upset many in Ethiopia and Israel. As anti-Semitism grew in Ethiopia, some of the Jewish community converted to Christianity to protect themselves. These converts, estimated today to be in the hundreds, aren't recognized as Jews by the Israeli government. Many have relatives already in Israel and can apply for citizenship on that basis. However, critics say this isn't good enough.

In 1985, Ethiopian Jews successfully protested against the Chief Rabbinate's demand they go through a symbolic conversion to Judaism, and the Rabbinate dropped the requirement.

Russian-born Oleg made aliyah with his family when he was just 8 years old. Today, he is an entrepreneur in Israel's lively and booming high-tech industry.

CHAPTER 3
The Accidental Israeli

Oleg was eight years old when his parents decided the family (he and his younger sister) would move to Israel.[1] It wasn't his first move. Years earlier, the family had already left Russia, where Oleg was born, to live in Moldova. At the time, both Russia and Moldova were within the Soviet Union. Life was good for Oleg. He enjoyed school, friends, and fishing in the river near his home.

He didn't really know he was Jewish. Officially, the Soviet Union was an **atheist** country. Oleg wasn't raised with any Jewish religious tradition. His grandparents spoke Yiddish, a language that European Jews spoke for centuries. It has elements of Hebrew, German and other Central and Eastern European languages. He heard stories about anti-Semitism from his parents and grandparents, but he had never experienced it himself.

When the Soviet Union fell apart in late 1991, Oleg's parents packed up the family and left for Israel. It didn't mean much to Oleg that they were going to Israel. He was just excited about the new adventure. The family had traveled through many parts of Russia for vacations, so for Oleg this was just another plane ride to a new place.

The transition to Israeli life was a challenge for Oleg and his family. His parents had trouble finding jobs in their professions. They didn't speak the language. At the time, Oleg and his family were among the nearly one million Russian-speaking immigrants

A flight of Russian immigrants, arriving in 1995, is welcomed at Israel's Ben-Gurion airport by then-chair of the Jewish Agency, Avraham Burg.

A young immigrant family from the Soviet Union goes through the paperwork of gaining their new citizenship at Israel's airport (1971).

who came to Israel during the 1990s. In 1990, Israel's population was only 4.8 million[2], and by 2000, Israel's population had grown to 6.4 million.[3] The country and the economy weren't quite ready to absorb so many new citizens. Like many other immigrants, Oleg's parents took the jobs they could find, but their work did not provide the same standard of living he had been used to in Moldova.

Grammar school was also difficult. One teacher tried to rename him "Alex." There were only six other Russians at his school, and they fought almost daily with the Israeli boys. His family eventually moved to Ashdod, a southern port city along the Mediterranean Sea. They moved there because the Israeli government had built low-cost apartments for new immigrants.

The Accidental Israeli

Ashdod is located on Israel's southern coast along the Mediterranean Sea. One of Israel's largest cities, it is home to one of the country's busiest ports.

Many Russians moved there, and Oleg says that today you can still speak Russian almost anywhere in town and be understood.

Oleg's life changed a great deal once he began high school. His parents sent him to attend high school in Rehovot (reh-HOE-vote), a city just outside Tel Aviv. They believed this high school would give him better academic opportunities. Oleg had known he wanted to be a software engineer since he hacked his first computer game during grammar school. At this

Rehovot is a mid-size city to the south of Tel Aviv, in the center of Israel. A diverse city with a mix of religious and secular Jews, Rehovot also has sizable populations of Russian, Yemenite, Ethiopian, and **Anglo** backgrounds. It's also the location of the Weizmann Institute of Science.

high school, he could study as much math, physics, and software engineering as he could fit into his schedule—and he managed to fit in quite a lot.

Leaving Ashdod and his Russian-speaking community gave Oleg his first expanded experience of Israeli culture. His classmates included both Israelis who were born in the country and olim from other parts of the world. Unlike the children in his first Israeli school, in Rehovot, everyone worked well together and got along. Oleg says, "We had the feeling that nobody was on the outside."

Today Oleg is an **entrepreneur**. He is in charge of a technology and agriculture company. Yet he is still not sure how he feels about calling himself an Israeli. He believes that technology and the internet are making the world so small that labels like nationality or religion won't matter in the future. Yet, he still feels Israeli when he travels overseas as part of his job.

Visiting other countries helps him see cultural differences more clearly. He finds the Asian countries he visits more formal and more **hierarchial** than Israeli culture. When he visits the United States, the young Americans he meets seem less serious about their lives and their future than Israelis the same age. That may be because most young Israelis serve in the army and that experience makes them more mature. So even though Oleg doesn't like labels, he has discovered that cultural differences still have meaning.

Oleg believes that Israeli culture is particularly suitable for creating new technologies. Because of Israel's lack of formality and hierarchy, people feel free to experiment with new ideas. Israelis aren't so worried they'll look bad if things don't work out. Oleg explains, "You can't really fail in Israel. In other cultures, if you fall short of what you plan to achieve, you might lose people's respect. In Israel, if you fail, nobody really cares. It just means there's something else to try."

THE LIFE ADVENTURES OF A RUSSIAN ACTIVIST

Before the fall of the Soviet Union in 1991, it was very difficult for anyone to leave, especially for Jews. There were people who wanted to live elsewhere, so they could have more rights and freedom. The Soviet Government considered it **treasonous** even to apply for permission to leave the country. Requests for permission to leave went unanswered for years, and even then most were denied. The individuals who were refused the right to leave were called "refuseniks."

One of the country's most famous refusniks was Anatoly Sharansky, who changed his first name to Natan. He was a leader among Jews and non-Jews in the Soviet Union, a **communist** country. He, alongside others, led the fight for human rights. In 1973, Natan applied for a **visa** to move to Israel, and his request was denied. He protested the unfair way that refuseniks were treated by the government. He was arrested for his activism by the Soviet authorities in 1977.

In 1978, he was convicted of being a spy for the United States and sentenced to prison for 13 years. Before the court announced its verdict, Natan proclaimed, "To the court I have nothing to say—to my wife and the Jewish people I say 'Next Year in Jerusalem.'"[4]

He spent nine years in a hard labor camp, where he was tortured. Natan was eventually released as part of a Soviet-American prisoner swap.

Natan finally realized his dream of moving to Israel on the same day he was released from prison. Once in Israel, Natan continued his **activist** life. He no longer had to fear the government would arrest him for giving voice to his opinions. He became a member of Knesset in 1996, where he served until 2006. During this period, he was also a deputy prime minister under four different governments.

Today Natan is chairman of The Jewish Agency, an organization dedicated to helping Jews all over the world make the move to Israel.

Natan Sharansky

California-native Lela Gilbert shares her story as a Christian resident of Israel and the Middle East.

CHAPTER 4
"Sunday People"

She never meant to stay in Israel this long. Lela Gilbert came to Jerusalem for a four-month visit in 2006 and simply never left.[1] She moved to a new neighborhood at some point during her eight years in Jerusalem. However, she says she's not yet ready to return to her native California, although she still visits regularly. Will she go back? Perhaps someday. But not today.

Lela's arrival in Israel eight years ago was the first time she'd ever set foot in the country. Her father had long dreamed of visiting Israel and he shared his fascination with the small, faraway country with his daughter. Unfortunately, Lela's father died before he could make his trip. So Lela made the trip for him, and to explore her religious roots as a Christian. "I came on a pilgrimage. The holy places of Judaism and Christianity represent road signs and revelations in my own spiritual journey."[2]

Her interest in Israel isn't purely spiritual. Lela's been studying and writing about the persecution of Christians in the Middle East for years. She came to Israel to see a different side of the Middle East, one where "Christians, Jews and Muslims live more or less side-by-side . . . I imagined that living in a country where these religious groups area represented—even amidst tension and occasional terror—would give me a more intimate and direct experience of that reality."[3]

As a practical matter, Lela's transition to life in Israel was fairly easy. Her children back in California are grown. They had

CHAPTER 4

encouraged her to try something different from life she knew so well in Orange County. She's a professional writer and fortunate to be able to continue the work she did back in the United States. Learning the language was not essential. As she describes it, her Hebrew is "**atrocious**."

The good news is that her lack of Hebrew skills hasn't kept her from enjoying the easy, **spontaneous** sociability and hospitality of Israelis. Lela finds the openness of Israelis is one of the best qualities of the country's culture. When she was moving into her new apartment in Jerusalem, neighbors stopped her on the steps and invited her over for a glass of wine. Lela hesitated. She was used to her California neighbors saying they should all get together, but never quite making it happen. It was time to do things differently in her new country. She accepted.

Lela considers her Christian faith an important and essential part of her life and has never felt like an outsider in the Jewish state. Her Israeli friends invite her to their family celebrations, Sabbath dinners, and other holiday gatherings. Lela loves to participate in these events and believes they're all a part of what she calls the "wonderful, life-affirming spirit of Israel's people." She adds, "Israelis celebrate life. And I love celebrating it with them!"

None of this means she leaves her Christian faith behind. Like other Christians who live in Israel, Sunday is her Sabbath, and in that way, she and other "Sunday People" are different from Jewish Israelis who observe Friday night and Saturday as the day of rest. Lela sometimes attends one of Jerusalem's churches and enjoys listening to Christian music. Most Israelis don't celebrate Christmas, but Lela says that for Christians, Christmas in Israel is less about gifts and more about the spirit of the holy day. Observing Easter in Jerusalem has been particularly meaningful for Lela.

Christian pilgrims to Israel recreate the steps of Jesus each Palm Sunday, when they walk from the Mount of Olives to Jerusalem's Old City.

The Via Dolorosa winds from Lions' Gate at the walls of Jerusalem's Old City to the Church of the Holy Sepulchre inside the Old City. On Good Friday, Christians from all over the world join in a procession along this path, believed to be the one Jesus walked to his crucifixion.

Lela does miss Mexican and Southwestern American food, which isn't so popular in Israel. Limes are only available in Israel for a few weeks each summer, which makes it difficult for Lela to prepare her own Southwestern fare. Israel grows most of its own food, so the fresh fruits and vegetables sold in local grocery stores are only those available in season. She's also not quite yet comfortable measuring her ingredients according to the metric system, as Israelis do.

These are just minor challenges. Throughout the rest of the Middle East, the persecution of Christians is becoming more frequent and more violent. Lela is grateful to live in Israel with its "authentic religious freedom," among a "Christian population [that] is safe and thriving."[4]

ISRAEL'S CHRISTIAN VISITORS

More than 3.5 million tourists visited Israel in 2013, and most of them were Christians.[5] The United States and Russia send the most Christian tourists. Many also come from European countries, as well as Latin American countries such as Brazil.[6] Around 40 percent of these visitors describe themselves as pilgrims who visit Israel for religious reasons.[7]

Most Christian visitors, even those who don't define themselves as pilgrims, visit Christian sites. In Jerusalem, these sites include the Church of the Holy Sepulchre (Sehe-pull-ker), where Jesus is believed to have been buried, and the Mount of Olives, where he spoke. The vast majority of Christians also visit the Church of the Nativity in Bethlehem, which is under Palestinian control.

Inside the Church of the Holy Sepulchre on the Saturday before Easter. Orthodox Christians participate in the Holy Fire ceremony.

They also visit northern Israel, where most of Israel's native Christians live. One of the most popular Christian sites in the north is the small town of Capernaum (CAP-pehr-nai-uhm) on the northern tip of the Sea of Galilee. Israelis call this lake the *Kinneret* (kee-nair-REHT). It is a site where Jesus once lived, and the town is also home to the remains of an ancient **synagogue** and an ancient church.

The "Gospel Trail" is a hiking trail that runs nearly 40 miles, connecting Nazareth to the Kinneret. It's meant to give people a chance to "walk" in the footsteps of Jesus. With beautiful nature all around, some people choose to ride along the trail on rented bikes or horses instead.

Christian communities have created a number of sites to help visitors learn more about the local history and culture. One of the newest is the International Center of Mary of Nazareth. This center is run by Israel's French Catholic Community. They hope the center will foster unity among Christians and people of all religions.

Tania traces her family background from Tunisia to France, and now has moved with her children to Israel.

CHAPTER 5
The Beauty of a Challenging Life

Tania and her family were already well established in Paris.[1] In the 1960s, both her parents and her husband's immigrated to France from the North African country of Tunisia. They had made a good life for their children in Paris. About a decade ago, Tania and her husband, with a three-year-old boy and a baby girl just six months old, decided to leave their comfortable life in Paris and move to Israel.

Why did they make the move? They wanted their children to grow up in a country where they could enjoy a strong Jewish community and culture, even if they didn't practice all the rituals of their religion. Many of Tania's husband's Tunisian relatives had immigrated to Israel. They were familiar with the country and they knew that Israel could be a Jewish home for both religious and **secular** Jews. Once they made the decision to move to Israel, they immigrated within six months.

Like so many other new immigrants to Israel, Tania began studying at *ulpan* (ool-pahn), a special, intensive Hebrew course. The Israeli government provides six months of free ulpan classes for all new immigrants. Tania says it took her a few years to become fluent. She also joined a choir to practice Hebrew and meet friends.

After studying Hebrew at a local ulpan, Tania found it a challenge to find a job that matched her French education and professional experience. Tania was drawn to the excitement of

Inside of El Ghriba synagogue in Tunisia. This current synagogue was built in the nineteenth century on the site of other synagogues destroyed over the centuries. Tradition holds that one of the stones in an arch of El Ghriba is from the First Temple in Jerusalem, brought by Jews fleeing the Babylonians.

Israel's high-tech industry, and hoped she could contribute her knowledge and experience in a new job.

She had earned a master's degree from a well-known French university and had a successful career with a technology company in France. But Israeli employers weren't familiar with her background, so it took some time to find a job. Eventually, Tania was hired by an Israeli who had worked in France and understood the value of her qualifications. Once she got her foothold in the Israeli high-tech world and became fluent in Hebrew, her career advanced. Now she has a senior executive

Paris, France

The Beauty of a Challenging Life

position in global marketing at a major Israeli software company. She also volunteers with an organization that helps other immigrants get established in Israel.

She enjoys the swift pace of Israeli business, especially in comparison to the business culture in France. Tania says that in France, businesses set up lots of committees for discussions and research before anything is decided and done. In Israel, if someone has an idea to do something—they do it. Tania says she's been able to raise her children in the type of Jewish community she'd hoped. Her children participated in activities typical of Israeli children, such as camping and dancing. She remembers that when she grew up in France, her life was more restricted and most of her free time was spent on homework. Tania is glad her children were able to enjoy greater freedom and time with friends.

She notes that during parent-teacher meetings, the first questions teachers asked were how the children were doing socially: did they feel accepted, did they have friends? The

Israeli children building a bonfire on Lag Ba'Omer, a spring festival celebrated with bonfires and nature hikes throughout Israel. The holiday celebrates, among other events, the renewal of hope in the aftermath of a second century plague in ancient Israel.

teachers moved on to discuss their grades only after talking about their social well-being.

Like many secular Israeli Jews, Tania's family has its own way of observing Shabbat. They say *kiddush* (kee-DOOSH), the Sabbath prayer over wine, on Friday night before sitting down to a big family dinner. Rather than go to synagogue, they are more likely to go to a movie after dinner.

Today, the two young children they brought to Israel are serving in the Israeli army. Her son is in a special military program, which includes studying computer science at a leading Israeli university. Her daughter is going into the air force. Tania admits that it is not easy to send her children off to the army, but they are both eager to take on the challenge. Serving in the Israeli military is part of being a member of the community, and it also creates opportunities for their future careers.

And for Tania, it's this combination of challenge and community that pulled her to Israel. She thinks of Israel's early pioneers, and the spirit and motivation they needed to get through the toughest times in order to found a modern state. In France, life was easy compared to Israel, but they did not have the same sense of community there. Tania says that in Israel, "We want to do more than have a nice individual life. You come to Israel that's still growing, and you feel committed to Israel. It's not like moving to another country. We're Jewish, it's our country; we feel that attachment."

Home Front Command soldiers as they finish their training to become rescue specialists (2014).

A CHAPTER IN FRENCH HISTORY— THE DREYFUS AFFAIR

In 1893, Lieutenant Colonel Alfred Dreyfus (dry-foos) was accused and convicted of treason by a military court in France. He was a Jew, and anti-Semitism and faked evidence both played a role in convicting him. He was sentenced to life imprisonment on Devil's Island prison. His official sentence including a public humiliation: he was stripped of his medals and honors, his uniform, and his sword during a military ceremony. The crowd, including army officers and the public, shouted anti-Semitic slurs at him. One newspaper wrote that he was not even French. The publisher stated: Dreyfus "committed no crime against his country. To betray one's country, one must first have one."[2]

Alfred Dreyfus

Dreyfus's trial changed the life of Theodor Herzl (hair-tzul), a Hungarian-born Jew who was a journalist who wrote about the trial. Herzl wrote that "the shattering impact"[3] of the trial had a great influence on him, and in 1895 he wrote a book called *The Jewish State*.

In *The Jewish State*, Herzl argued that European anti-Semitism would always prevent Jews from being accepted, and that the Jews should build a new state in their ancient homeland. An assimilated European Jew himself, Herzl saw how another assimilated Jew, one who'd fought for his country, was still subjected to cruel anti-semitism.

Theodor Herzl

Unfortunately, many of Europe's Jews are again experiencing a **relentless** wave of violent anti-Semitism, including in France. Many Jews in France now say they won't wear anything that can identify them as Jews for fear of attack. This spike of anti-Semitism is cited as one of the reasons French aliyah has also spiked.[4]

Iranian-born, Israeli singer and actress Rita performing at a live concert in Jerusalem in 2009.

CHAPTER 6
From Tehran to Tel Aviv

Legally, her name is Rita Hayan-Feruz Kleinstein. To her millions of fans around the world, she's simply Rita. She's a pop singer who has been recording best-selling music in Israel for decades. She is also an actress who won the Israeli film industry's "Actress of the Year" award in 1989. Decades later in 2008, Israelis voted Rita as their number one singer during the country's sixtieth anniversary festivities. Rita is a beloved national symbol. The Iranian-born Israeli superstar has represented Israel on the international stage and been front and center for many national celebrations.

During Israel's special **Jubilee** fiftieth anniversary in 1998, Rita sang the national anthem, *Hatikvah* (ha-TEEK-vah) at the official national ceremony. In 2013, she performed at the General Assembly of the United Nations during an event called "Tunes for Peace." She sang in Hebrew, English, and in her first language—Farsi (far-see), the language spoken in Iran.

Rita was born in Tehran (tay-RON), Iran in 1962. She was eight years old when her family fled Iran. Just nine years later in 1979, there was a revolution in Iran. For many years, Iran had been ruled as a secular **monarchy**, but the leadership was taken over by very strong-minded religious leaders and became an Islamic **theocracy**. Even during the years before the 1979 revolution, Iran's Muslim majority didn't always treat its Jewish minority well. Rita and her family lived in a Muslim neighborhood in Tehran and went to a Muslim school. She recalls her parents

Tehran is Iran's capital and largest city. It is located between the Alborz Mountains to its north and the desert to its south.

telling her and her siblings that they shouldn't tell people they were Jewish. It was safer to blend in.

One day at school, a teacher called on Rita's older sister to recite the Muslim morning prayer. Rita's sister didn't know the prayer and said so. When the girls told their parents what had happened, Rita remembers her father making a life-changing decision right then and there. "That's it, I think we need to leave for our homeland," he said.[1]

The family left Tehran for Israel. When they arrived, they stayed with relatives for a couple of weeks. Eventually, they moved to a house in Ramat Hasharon (rah-MAHT ha-SHA-rown), not far from Tel Aviv. This is where Rita grew up. She described the move as scary. It was difficult to leave everything and everyone she knew. Today, she is no longer afraid of new and different people and situations. She delights in the tapestry of Israel. "We, the Jewish people, are after all, a million puzzle pieces representing places around the world, trying to create a new picture put together miraculously. I think that is the beauty of our country."[2]

New immigrants in a ma'abara (ma-ah-bah-rah), one of the temporary tent cities set up by Israel starting in 1950, to absorb the high number olim arriving to the young country. The population in ma'abarot started to decline in 1953, as the olim became absorbed into the general Israeli population. In some cases, the ma'abarot themselves were turned into permanent neighborhoods or towns.

Her love for Israel doesn't mean she's forgotten the Iran of her childhood. In 2011, for the first time, she released an album in which all the songs were in Farsi. *Hasmachot Sheli* (ha-sma-KHOT sheh-LEE) or "My Joys" in English, is filled with classic Persian songs.

These days, Rita's music is playing throughout Iran, as well as other Muslim countries such as Turkey and Lebanon. But in Iran, the Islamic regime has outlawed all music it doesn't approve. Music stores in Iran can't openly sell her album, so they do it quietly with a blank album cover that only shows the name "Miss Rita." Her fans in Muslim countries know exactly who she is and that she is Israeli. They know the risks they face for just downloading her music or buying her album. They're taking that risk. She hears from her Iranian fans by email and on Facebook.

CHAPTER 6

Rita performs at a State Dinner before Prime Minister Benjamin Netanyahu and US President Barack Obama on March 21, 2013. She sings Yerushalayim shel Zahav (yeh-roo-shah-lie-eem shel zah-hav), which means "Jerusalem of Gold." One of Israel's most popular and patriotic songs, it describes the longing of the Jews to return to Jerusalem and celebrates the city's reunification in 1967.

Rita says she dreams of a day when she can sing her songs in Iran. Right now, the Iranian regime doesn't allow Israelis to enter the country. Even though she can't visit Iran, her music is a bridge between Iran and Israel, two of the Middle East's most ancient communities. The two nations have had ties at various times during the past two thousand years. Despite the huge challenges today, Rita hopes one day "there will be peace and I'm going to sing there [Iran]."[3]

HIDDEN JEWS

In many places throughout time, Jews lived in communities where they had to hide their Jewish identity to remain safe. One such community was Mashad (mah-shahd), a town in northeastern Iran. In 1839, the Jewish community there was attacked with a horrible **pogrom**. Many Jews were killed. Those who survived were given two choices: convert to Islam or die.

They "converted" to stay alive, but quietly kept up Jewish practices. They'd light Shabbat candles under cover so they couldn't be seen.

Jews living in the Soviet Union who wanted to learn Hebrew or practice Judaism also had to do it under the watchful eye of the government or in secret.

Another group of hidden Jews are the "Conversos" (cone-vehr-sos) whose origins are in Spain and Portugal. The Jews who became known as Conversos began to convert to Christianity in the late fourteenth century. They too kept Jewish practices as best they could, while outwardly practicing Catholicism. It was so dangerous for anyone to discover they were Jewish that the family members who knew didn't even tell the next generation about their Jewish identity. Soon, it was left to the women in the family to quietly keep Jewish traditions in the home and pass them down only to their daughters.

Today, their descendants are only starting to learn of their heritage. Organizations now exist to help trace their roots. The founder of one such organization is Rabbi Yosef Garcia (Yo-sef Gar-see-ah). Once he discovered his Jewish background, he said that his grandmother's ritual of lighting candles on Friday night finally started to make sense.[4]

The lighting of Shabbat candles.

CHAPTER NOTES

Introduction

1. Shmuel Trigano. "The Expulsion of the Jews from Muslim Countries, 1920–1970: A History of Ongoing Cruelty and Discrimination," Jerusalem Center for Public Affairs, November 4, 2010. http://jcpa.org/article/the-expulsion-of-the-jews-from-muslim-countries-1920-1970-a-history-of-ongoing-cruelty-and-discrimination/

Chapter 1: Two Sisters; Two Countries

1. Rachel, Michal, and Shira (mother and her two daughters; immigrants from the United States), interview with the author, April 8, 2014.

2. Erin McClam. "Americans fight for Israel as 'Lone Soldiers' in Gaza Strip," NBCnews.com, July 22, 2014. http://www.nbcnews.com/storyline/middle-east-unrest/americans-fight-israel-lone-soldiers-gaza-strip-n161441

3. Diana Bruk. "Hard core of new immigrant soldiers is ready to serve," *The Times of Israel*, August 14, 2014. http://www.timesofisrael.com/hard-core-of-new-immigrant-soldiers-is-ready-to-serve/

Chapter 2: A Dangerous Journey

1. Raphael Ahren. "Teshome Solomon's arduous, triumphant trek to the Knesset," *The Times of Israel*, April 16, 2013. http://www.timesofisrael.com/teshome-solomons-arduous-triumphant-trek-to-the-knesset/

2. Mitchell Ginsburg. "Battling to integrate: The IDF's misunderstood Ethiopian recruits." *The Times of Israel*, May 1, 2014. http://www.timesofisrael.com/battling-to-integrate-the-idfs-misunderstood-ethiopian-recruits/

Chapter 3: The Unintentional Israeli

1. Oleg (immigrant from Russia), interview with author, July 2, 2014.

2. Central Bureau of Statistics, Israel "The population of Israel 1999-2009," http://unstats.un.org/unsd/wsd/docs/Israel_wsd_brochure.pdf

3. Ibid.

4. The Jewish Agency. "Natan Sharanksy: Chairman of the Executive." http://www.jewishagency.org/executive-members/natan-sharansky-0

CHAPTER NOTES

Chapter 4: "Sunday People"
    1. Lela Gilbert (Israeli resident from the United States), email correspondence with the author, July 29, 2014.
    2. Lela Gilbert, *Saturday People, Sunday People: Israel Through the Eyes of a Christian Sojourner* (New York: Encounter Books, 2012), p. viii.
    3. Ibid.
    4. Lela Gilbert. "Christians in the Crosshairs," *Hadassah Magazine*, August/September 2014. http://www.hadassahmagazine.org/2014/09/08/christians-crosshairs/
    5. Israel Ministry of Foreign Affairs. "Christian tourism to Israel 2013." http://mfa.gov.il/MFA/PressRoom/2014/Pages/Christian-tourism-to-Israel-2013.aspx
    6. Ibid.
    7. Ibid.

Chapter 5: The Beauty of a Challenging Life
    1. Tania (immigrant from France), interview with author, June 11, 2014.
    2. Conor Cruise O'Brien. *The Siege*. New York: Simon & Schuster, 1986, page 64.
    3. Ibid, p. 65.
    4. Josh Hasten. "French anti-semitism and French aliyah skyrocket on parallel tracks." JNS.org, April 7, 2014. http://www.jns.org/latest-articles/2014/4/7/french-anti-semitism-and-french-aliyah-skyrocket-on-parallel-tracks#.U_CH8UsudMJ=

Chapter 6: From Tehran to Tel Aviv
    1. Jewish Agency. "From Iran to Israel with Love: Queen Rita's Own Aliyah Story." March 25, 2014. http://www.jewishagency.org/blog/1/article/12651
    2. Ibid.
    3. Elise Labot. CNN.com, "Rita: An Israeli star singing Iranian songs." September 13, 2012. http://edition.cnn.com/2012/09/11/world/meast/israeli-singer-rita-iran/
    4. Stuart Thornton. "Hidden History: Rabbi Explains the Identity of the Crypto-Jews." *National Geographic*, http://www.nationalgeographic.com/hidden-history/

WORKS CONSULTED

Ackerman, Gwen. "Banned Israel Singer Rita Woos Iranians Amid Attack Fear." *Bloomberg Businessweek*, August 20, 2012. http://www.businessweek.com/news/2012-08-20/banned-israel-singer-rita-woos-iranians-amid-attack-fear

Ahren, Raphael. "Teshome Solomon's arduous, triumphant trek to the Knesset." *The Times of Israel*, April 16, 2013. http://www.timesofisrael.com/teshome-solomons-arduous-triumphant-trek-to-the-knesset/

Amado, Melissa I. "The Descendants of Conversos: A Comparative Discussion of Practices." *Southwest Jewish Archives*, 1997. http://swja.arizona.edu/content/descendants-conversos-comparative-discussion-practices-melissa-i-amado

Basri, Carole. "The Jewish Refugees from Arab Countries: An Examination of Legal Rights—A Case Study of the Human Rights Violations of Iraqi Jews." *Fordham International Law Journal*, vol. 26, issue 3, 2002. http://ir.lawnet.fordham.edu/cgi/viewcontent.cgi?article=1881&context=ilj

Berger, Miriam. "The Last Jews of Ethiopia." *The Forward*, August 9, 2013. http://forward.com/articles/181857/the-last-jews-of-ethiopia/?p=all

Biography.com. "Alfred Dreyfus." http://www.biography.com/people/alfred-dreyfus-9279233#synopsis

Blum, Ruthie. "Christian tourists welcomed to the Holy Land," Israel21c.com, December 23, 2013. http://www.israel21c.org/travel/christian-tourists-welcomed-to-the-holy-land/

Bruk, Diana. "Hard core of new immigrant soldiers is ready to serve." *The Times of Israel*, August 14, 2014. http://www.timesofisrael.com/hard-core-of-new-immigrant-soldiers-is-ready-to-serve/

Cruise O'Brien, Conor. *The Siege: The Saga of Israel and Zionism*. New York: Simon & Schuster, 1986.

Eldar, Shlomi. "Jews from Arab countries: the forgotten refugees." *Al-Monitor*, November 22, 2013. http://www.al-monitor.com/pulse/originals/2013/11/un-conference-jews-arab-countries-refugees-negotiations.html#

Englander, David, ed. *The Jewish Enigma*. London, U.K.: Peter Halban Publishers, 1992.

Facts on File. "Natan Sharansky." http://www.fofweb.com/History/MainPrintPage.asp?iPin=ENJ0633&DataType=WorldHistory&WinType=Free

Fisher, Gabe. "All the kingmaker's men, and women." *The Times of Israel*, January 23, 2013. http://www.timesofisrael.com/yair-lapids-sends-a-diverse-quality-slate-to-knesset/

Frenkel, Sheera. "Iran to Israel and Back to Iran: Rita's Music Goes Home." NPR.org, November 12, 2012. http://www.npr.org/blogs/therecord/2012/11/12/164960099/iran-to-israel-and-back-to-iran-ritas-music-goes-home

WORKS CONSULTED

Friends of Yemin Order. "Graduates Giving Back: Simon Solomon." http://www.yeminorde.org/index.php/2012-01-28-09-33-17/80-success-stories/252-graduates-giving-back--simon-solomon

Expatica.com. "A guide to Spanish citizenship and permanent visas." May 23, 2014. http://www.expatica.com/es/essentials_moving_to/essentials/How-to-become-a-Spanish-national_18245.html

Gaunt, Doram. "Looney over limes," *The Times of Israel*, August 14, 2008. http://www.haaretz.com/looney-over-limes-1.251809

German Federal Office for Migration and Refugees. "Ethnic German resettlers." April 28, 2011. http://www.bamf.de/EN/Migration/Spaetaussiedler/spaetaussiedler-node.html

Gilbert, Lela. Email interview with author, July 29, 2014.

Ginsburg, Mitchell. "Battling to integrate: The IDF's misunderstood Ethiopian recruits." *The Times of Israel*, May 1, 2014. http://www.timesofisrael.com/battling-to-integrate-the-idfs-misunderstood-ethiopian-recruits/

Gladstone, Rick. "Many Seek Spanish Citizenship Offered to Sephardic Jews." *New York Times*, March 19, 2014. http://www.nytimes.com/2014/03/20/world/europe/many-seek-spanish-citizenship-offered-to-sephardic-jews.html

Greenfield, Murray S. and Joseph M. Hochstein. *The Jews' Secret Fleet*. Jerusalem: Gefen Publishing House, 2010.

Haaretz. "95% of Israelis believe racism is a problem." March 17, 2014. http://www.haaretz.com/news/national/1.580293

———. "Iranian-born Israeli pop star Rita to sing at UN General Assembly event." March 5, 2013. http://www.haaretz.com/life/culture/iranian-born-israeli-pop-star-rita-to-sing-at-un-general-assembly-event-1.507488

Halevy Donin, Rabbi Hayim. *To Pray as a Jew*. New York: Basic Books, 1991.

Harris, Emily. "Last Flight of Ethiopia-to-Israel Jewish Migration Program." NPR.org, September 1, 2013. http://www.npr.org/2013/09/01/217356628/last-flight-of-ethiopia-to-israel-jewish-migration-program

Hasten, Josh. "French anti-semitism and French aliyah skyrocket on parallel tracks." JNS.org, April 7, 2014. http://www.jns.org/latest-articles/2014/4/7/french-anti-semitism-and-french-aliyah-skyrocket-on-parallel-tracks#.U-utGFYudMI=

History.com. "Alfred Dreyfus." http://www.history.com/topics/alfred-dreyfus

Hoare, Liam. "Rising Number of French Jews Making Aliyah." *Tablet*, December 30, 2013. http://www.tabletmag.com/scroll/157703/rising-number-of-french-jews-making-aliyah

Israel Central Bureau of Statistics. "The population of Israel 1990-2009." October 20, 2010. https://unstats.un.org/unsd/wsd/docs/Israel_wsd_brochure.pdf

WORKS CONSULTED

IDF Info. "Nefesh b'Nefesh." http://www.idfinfo.co.il/Nefesh_B_Nefesh.php?cat=a11

Israel Knesset. "Shimon Solomon." https://www.knesset.gov.il/mk/eng/mk_eng.asp?mk_individual_id_t=883

Israel Ministry of Foreign Affairs. "Christian tourism to Israel 2013." http://mfa.gov.il/MFA/PressRoom/2014/Pages/Christian-tourism-to-Israel-2013.aspx

Jewish Agency. "From Iran to Israel with Love: Queen Rita's Own Aliyah Story." March 25, 2014. http://www.jewishagency.org/blog/1/article/12651

———. "Law of Return." http://www.jewishagency.org/first-steps/program/5131

———. "Natan Sharanksy: Chairman of the Executive." http://www.jewishagency.org/executive-members/natan-sharansky-0

———. "Refusniks." http://jafi.org/JewishAgency/English/About/Profile/Chairman/Refuseniks.htm

Jewish Virtual Library. "Israel: Immigration to Israel." http://www.jewishvirtuallibrary.org/jsource/Immigration/immigtoc.html

Labot, Elise. "Rita: An Israeli star singing Iranian songs." CNN.com, September 13, 2012. http://edition.cnn.com/2012/09/11/world/meast/israeli-singer-rita-iran/

Lewis, Bernard. *The Middle East: A Brief History of the Last 2,000 Years*. New York: Scribner, 1995.

Lewis, Bernard. *The Shaping of the Modern Middle East*. New York: Oxford University Press, 1994.

Lior, Ilan. "Israel expands Law of Return to apply to non-Jewish same-sex spouses." *Haaretz*, August 12, 2014. http://www.haaretz.com/news/national/.premium-1.610157

Lone Soldier Center. "Who Are Lone Soldiers?" http://lonesoldiercenter.com/about-us/who-are-lone-soldiers/

Mark, Jonathan. "Rebel Purims Lead Russian Passover." *The Jewish Week*, April 24, 2014. http://www.thejewishweek.com/news/new-york/rebel-purims-lead-russian-passover

McClam, Erin. "Americans Fight for Israel as 'Lone Soldiers' in Gaza." NBCnews.com, July 22, 2014. http://www.nbcnews.com/storyline/middle-east-unrest/americans-fight-israel-lone-soldiers-gaza-strip-n161441

Meron, Ya'akov. "Why Jews Fled the Arab Countries." *The Middle East Quarterly*, September 1995, pp. 45–47. http://www.meforum.org/263/why-jews-fled-the-arab-countries

Middle East Quarterly. "Natan Sharansky: 'Peace will only come after Freedom and Democracy," Winter 2005, pp. 79–83. http://www.meforum.org/666/natan-sharansky-peace-will-only-come-after

WORKS CONSULTED

Namdar, Ruby. "Shabbat Recipes from Persia's 'Hidden Jews.'" *The Jewish Daily Forward*, April 24, 2013. http://blogs.forward.com/the-jew-and-the-carrot/175320/shabbat-recipes-from-persias-hidden-jews/

Oleg K. Phone interview with author, July 2, 2014.

Rita: Official Website. "Biography." http://www.rita.co.il/en/home/a/main/

Russo, Yocheved Miriam. "The double lives of Mashhadi Jews." *The Jerusalem Post*, August 22, 2007. http://www.jpost.com/Cafe-Oleh/Ask-The-Expert/The-double-lives-of-Mashhadi-Jews

Shaviv, Miriam. "Jewish by candlelight—from Spanish conversos to modern mixed marriage." *Haaretz*, May 8, 2009. http://www.haaretz.com/news/jewish-by-candlelight-from-spanish-converso-to-modern-mixed-marriage-1.275676

Shira and Michal M. In-person interview with author, April 8, 2014.

Sobelman, Batsheva. "Organized immigration of Ethiopian Jews to Israel ends." *The Los Angeles Times*, August 28, 2013. http://articles.latimes.com/2013/aug/28/world/la-fg-wn-israel-ethiopian-jews-20130828

Sokol, Sam. "Sharansky predicts 'beginning of the end of Jewish history in Europe," *The Jerusalem Post*, August 14, 2014. http://www.jpost.com/Diaspora/Sharansky-predicts-beginning-of-the-end-of-Jewish-history-in-Europe-371115

Strich, Joseph. "Jewish Agency chief touts anticipated wave of French olim." *The Jerusalem Post*, July 6, 2014. http://www.jpost.com/Jewish-World/Jewish-News/Jewish-Agency-chief-touts-anticipated-wave-of-French-olim-361614

Tania A. Phone interview with author, June 11, 2014.

Thornton, Stuart. "Hidden History: Rabbi Explains the Identity of the Crypto-Jews." *National Geographic*. http://www.nationalgeographic.com/hidden-history/

Trigano, Shmuel. "The Expulsion of the Jews from Muslim Countries, 1920-1970: A History of Ongoing Cruelty and Discrimination." Jerusalem Center for Public Affairs, November 4, 2010. http://jcpa.org/article/the-expulsion-of-the-jews-from-muslim-countries-1920-1970-a-history-of-ongoing-cruelty-and-discrimination/

Yaffe, Nurit, and Dorith Tal. "Immigration to Israel from the Former Soviet Union." Central Bureau of Statistics Israel. http://www.cbs.gov.il/statistical/immigration_e.pdf

Yesh Atid. "Our Agenda." http://en.yeshatid.org.il/Our-Agenda

Yiddish Scientific Institute. Basic Facts About Yiddish. New York: 1947. http://www.yivo.org/images/uploads/images/Basic%20Facts%20About%20Yiddish.pdf

Youth Aliyah Child Rescue. "Shimon Solomon: from survival to leadership." http://www.youthaliyah.org/events/shimon-solomon-from-survival-to-leadership

FURTHER READING

Jacobs Altman, Linda. *The Creation of Israel (World History Series)*. San Diego: Greenhaven Press, 1998.

Lehman Wilzig, Tami. *Passover Around the World*. Minneapolis: Kar-Ben Publishing, 2006.

Leiman, Sondra. *The Atlas of Great Jewish Communities: A Voyage Through History*. New York: URJ Press, 2002.

Sofer, Barbara. *Keeping Israel Safe: Serving in the Israel Defense Forces*. Minneapolis: Kar-Ben Publishing, 2008.

Speilman, Gloria. *Janusz Korczak's Children*. Minneapolis: Kar-Ben Publishing, 2007.

ON THE INTERNET

The Association of Crypto-Jews: The History of the Crypto-Jews/Hispanic Sephardi
http://www.cryptojew.org/the_history_of_the_beni_anusim.html

The Genesis Prize: Henrietta Szold
http://www.genesisprize.org/genesis-generation/celebrating-our-heritage/henrietta-szold.html

Time for Kids: Israel—A Day in the Life
http://www.timeforkids.com/destination/israel/day-in-life

Youth Aliyah Child Rescue: Our Villages
http://www.youthaliyah.org/villages/

Jewish Journal: L.A. Lone Soldiers honored by IDF
http://www.jewishjournal.com/los_angeles/article/l.a._lone_soldiers_honored_by_idf

PHOTO CREDITS: Design elements from Thinkstock and Dreamstime/Sharon Beck. Cover, p. 1—Rawpixelimages/Dreamstime; pp. 2–3 (background), 3–4, 33 (top), 40, 50—Thinkstock; p. 2 (map)—United Nations/Public Domain; p. 6—Berthold Werner/Public Domain; p. 7—House of Peace/cc-by-sa 3.0; p. 8—Jewish Agency for Israel/cc-by-sa 2.0; p. 10—The Palmach Archive via PikiWiki/Public Domain; p. 11—Eic413/Public Domain; pp. Rachel, Michal and Shira's mother; p. 16—Avi Ohayon/GPO/cc-by-sa 2.0; pp. 17, 45—Dnaveh/Dreamstime; p. 18—Stitchik/Dreamstime; p. 19—Ori Shifrin, IDF Spokesperson Film Unit/cc-by-sa 2.0; p. 20—Yesh Atid political party/cc-by-sa 3.0; p. 23—Government Press Office/cc-by-sa 2.0; pp. 24–25, 30–31—Israeli Tsvika/GPO/cc-by-sa 3.0; p. 26—Noam Chen/Israeli Ministry of Tourism/Israeli Parliament/cc-by-sa 2.0; p. 27—Harnik Nati/GPO/cc-by-sa 2.0; p. 28—Oleg; p. 32—Milner Moshe/GPO/cc-by-sa 2.0; p. 33 (bottom)—Amos Meron/WikiAir Israel/cc-by-sa 3.0; p. 35—Kira Sso/cc-by-sa 2.0; p. 36—Lela Gilbert; pp. 39, 41—Dafna Tal/GoIsrael.com; p. 42—Tania; p. 44 (top)—Citizen59/cc-by-sa 2.0, (bottom)—Michal Bednarek/Dreamstime; p. 46—IDF Spokesperson's Unit/c-by-sa 2.0; p. 47 (top)—George Eastman House Collection; p. 47 (bottom)—Imagno/Hulton Archive/Getty Images; p. 48—Itzik Edri/cc-by-sa 3.0; p. 51—Jewish Agency for Israel/cc-by-sa 2.0; p. 52—AFP Photo/Saul Loeb/AFP/Getty Images.

GLOSSARY

absorption center (uhb-zorp-shun sen-tear)—temporary housing the government of Israel provides to new immigrants, which often offer special services to new immigrants to help them ease into Israeli life

activist (ahk-tih-vist)—a person taking action intended to result in a political or social change, often as part of an organized group

airlift (ehr-lift)—moving people or supplies via air transportation during an emergency

Anglo (ayn-glow)—term used in Israel to describe immigrants coming from English-speaking countries

anti-semitism (an-tee-SEM-i-tiz-uhm)—discrimination against, or hatred of, Jews

assimilated (ah-sim-mill-ate-ehd)—to conform to the majority culture

atheist (EY-thee-ist)—a person who doesn't believe in the existence of God or gods

atrocious (ah-TROW-shus)—horrible

communist (kah-mew-neest)—a political and economic theory based on public ownership of all property and people's labor, requiring strict central control of people and society

distinction (diss-TINK-shun)—a difference

dubbed (duhb-bd)—when used regarding television or movies, it means to replace the dialogue with a different language from the original

entrepreneur (ahn-trih-PA-noor)—a person starting his or her own business

exclamation (ex-klah-MAY-shun)—a strong outcry

genocide (jeh-no-side)—the deliberate killing of a specific group of people, usually based on their ethnicity or culture

ghettos (geh-toes)—a term used by Venetians in the 16th century to describe the walled, dirty area within Venice where the Jews were forced to live; from that time, it was used to describe any area where governments forced Jews to live

Hashem (hah-SHEHM)—Hebrew for "the name," it's a term of respect religious Jews use in day-to-day (or "common" or "regular") speech to avoid breaking the commandment of taking the Lord's name in vain

hierarchical (hi-err-ARK-ih-kul)—a rigid order by rank

Holocaust (hah-low-cost)—refers to the systematic genocide inflicted on Jews by the Nazis during World War II

Holy Temple (hoh-lee tem-puhl)—Judaism's most sacred site; it refers to either of the two complexes in ancient in Jerusalem that where the center of Jewish religious ritual. The First Temple was destroyed in 586 BCE. The Second Temple was then built, but destroyed in 70 CE.

Jubilee (joo-buh-lee)—a special celebration mentioned in the Bible to occur every 50 years in Israel; has since become a term to describe any celebration or any sort of 50 year anniversary

GLOSSARY

Mossad (mow-sahd)—A shortened name for the Israeli government's agency for intelligence and special operations, similar to the CIA in the United States

monarchy (mahn-AR-key)—a form of government ruled by a head of state like a king or queen, selected from a royal family

olim (oh-LEEM)—Hebrew word for Jews who immigrate to Israel and become citizens; the singular is oleh (oh-LEH) for male immigrants and olah (oh-LAH) for female immigrants

ouster (OW-stir)—the removal or expulsion

paratroopers (pair-ah-troo-purhz)—soldiers trained to parachute from airplanes to their military missions

persecution (pur-sah-kwu-shun)—act of treating someone unfairly or cruelly based on a personal trait, such as religion or race

pogrom (pow-grawm)—a Yiddish word meaning "devastation," it was a term used to describe the attacks by Russian military against Jewish villages in the early 20th century; it has since become a term used to describe an organized attack by one group on another due to their ethnicity or culture

rabbi (RAB-ahy)—a Jewish religious leader who is ordained to perform Jewish rituals and make decisions regarding Jewish law

relentless (ree-lent-less)—persistent, without end

secular (SEK-yuh-ler)—not connected to a religion; in Israel it more precisely describes a lack of observance of religious law, but secular Israelis might still participate in Jewish traditions.

Shabbat (shah-BAHT)—the Jewish day of rest lasting 25 hours, starting roughly around sunset on Friday

spontaneous (spahn-tay-nee-us)—occur naturally and without prior planning

stealthy (stehl-thee)—done quietly to avoid being noticed

synagogue (sih-nah-gahg)—a Jewish house of worship

theocracy (thee-AH-crah-see)—a form of government ruled by religious authorities and based on religious doctrine

Torah (taw-RAH)—the first five books of the Jewish Bible

torture (tohr-chur)—causing extreme physical pain to another either as punishment or to force them to do or say something

treasonous (tree-zuhn-us)—betraying one's country; the crime of treason is usually defined as helping your country's enemies during a war

visa (vee-ZAH)—a document issued by a government that shows a non-citizen is present within its borders legally

viscious (vih-shus)—cruel and savage

Zionism (ZI-ohn—is-sohm)—the name given to the Jewish national movement to return to the Land of Israel, the ancient homeland of the Jewish people

INDEX

activities 15, 17, 18, 38, 43, 45
African refugees 22
aliyah 9, 10, 11, 13, 27, 28, 47
Aliyah Bet 10
anti-semitism 9, 10, 22, 27, 29, 47
Arab or Muslim countries 6, 11, 51
Muslims 27, 49, 50, 51
Ashdod 32, 33, 34
assimilation 9, 47
Babylonians 6, 44
Be'er Sheva 16, 22, 26
business culture 28, 34, 45
Canada 11
Christian holidays 38–40
Christianity 36, 37, 38, 40, 41, 53
communism 35
conversion, religious 27, 53
Dreyfus, Alfred 47
employment 29, 32, 34, 43, 44-45
entrepreneur 28, 34
Ethiopia 21, 22, 26, 27
Ethiopian Jews 9, 20, 21–27, 33
Europe 8, 9, 10, 29, 41, 47
food 18, 38, 40
France 8, 11, 42–47
French Revolution 9
friends 17, 18, 34, 38, 45
genocide 26
Great Assembly 7
Hamas 16, 19
Hebrew, learning 13, 15, 17, 22, 43, 53
Herzl, Theodor 47
Holocaust 22
Holy Temple 6, 7, 44
housing 15, 32, 51
IDF (military) 5, 19, 22, 34, 46, 47
Iran 49–53
Iranian Revolution 49
Israelites 6, 8
Jerusalem 6, 7, 15, 19, 26, 35, 37, 38, 39, 40, 41, 44, 48, 52
Jewish holidays 6, 38, 45
Judaism 7, 15, 27, 37, 53
Knesset 21, 26, 35
lone soldiers 19
Mediterranean Sea 10, 32, 33
Middle East 8, 9, 36, 37, 40, 52
Moldova 29, 32
North Africa 8, 9, 11, 43
North America 11
Operation Solomon 23, 27
organized immigration 8–11, 23–25, 27, 30–31, 35
Paris 43, 44, 45
Persians 6, 51
political motivation 9, 10
Rehovot 33, 34
religious motivation 8, 18, 21, 37
rockets 15, 16
Romans 6, 7
Russian Jews 9, 28, 31–35
schools 15, 22, 32, 33, 34, 44, 45, 50
Shabbat (Sabbath) 19, 22, 38, 46, 53
Sharansky, Natan 35
South American countries 41, 54
Soviet Union 9, 29, 32, 35, 53
Sudan 21, 22
Tel Aviv 33, 49, 50, 51
terror 15, 16, 19, 37
Thanksgiving 19
torture 22, 35
tourism 41
treason 35, 47
Tunisia 42, 43, 44
United Nations 49
United States 11, 13, 18, 34, 35, 38, 41
Yehuda Halevi, Rabbi 8
Yiddish 29
Zionism 9

About the Author

Elisa Silverman has written a number of books about Israel for Mitchell Lane Publishers. Originally from Chicago, Elisa began her own journey back to Israel as a teenager, touring the country for a summer. At the end of that summer, she decided to come back to Israel after she was graduated from college. Keeping that promise to herself, Elisa lived in Israel for a year in the early 1990s. She returned to the United States, but eventually the pull to return to Israel was too strong. Elisa made aliyah in 2002 and has been living in Jerusalem ever since. Today, she is a freelance writer with a focus on B2B content, but who also happily writes about other topics she loves (such as Israel).